Brainpower
smart
study

NINA SUNDAY

How to study
effectively using a
tested and proven
8-step method

First published in Australia in 2011 by:

Brainpower Training Pty Ltd,
Sydney, Australia.
HowToStudyMethod.com

Brainpower Smart Study™ is a trademark of Nina Sunday and Brainpower Training Pty Ltd.

The National Library of Australia
Cataloguing-in-Publication entry:

Sunday, Nina
Brainpower Smart Study: How to study effectively using a tested and proven 8-step method

ISBN 978 0 9751941 5 7

1. Study Skills – Handbook, Manuals, etc. 2. Active learning. I. Title
371.3

Cover design and internal layout and illustrations by Joy Lankshear
Edited by Helena Bond

Other Works
by Nina Sunday

Speed Reading training DVD   ISBN 978 0 9751941 0 2
Super Memory training DVD   ISBN 978 0 9751941 1 9
Customer Service training DVD   ISBN 978 0 9751941 2 6
Time Management training DVD   ISBN 978 0 9751941 3 3
Business Writing training DVD   ISBN 978 0 9751941 4 0

Nina Sunday, CSP*

BA, Dip Ed, Dip Arts (AustFilmTVSchl)

- Taught English and History at Caloundra High School, Queensland, and in Sydney High Schools, New South Wales, Australia.

- In 1990 founded Brainpower Training and pioneered Speed Reading and High Performance Memory training Australia-wide.

- Won an Innovation in Learning award from the Australian institute of Training and Development for Speed Reading training.

- Authored five training videos including 'Speed Reading' and 'Super Memory'.

* Certified Speaking Professional

Contents

Brainpower Smart Study 8-step method

1 – **Preview** for the big picture

2 – **Notes outline** using key headings

3 – **Read** for understanding

4 – **Reread** a little faster

5 – **Postview**

6 – **Start notes** – first from memory

7 – **Add notes** – open-book, use another colour

Take ten

8 – **Retell**

Standard version*

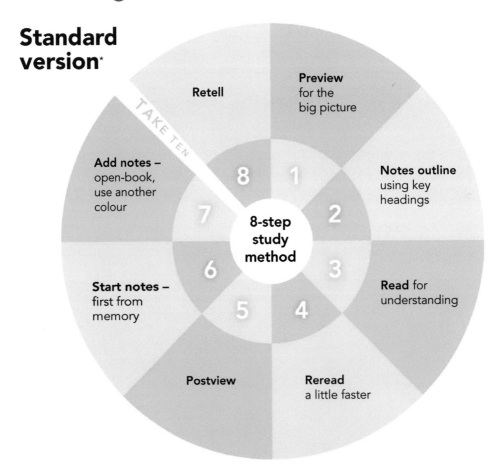

www.HowToStudyMethod.com

* Advanced version of the 8-step wheel incorporating memory mapping for notes is on page 49.

A first look at the Brainpower Smart Study 8-step method

Getting started

Estimate one manageable chunk of material to study. Don't select too big a chunk. Mark the beginning and end of your section to study with two paper clips*.

Step 1 | Preview for the big picture | 30 seconds – 1 minute

Preview for a minute or so, skimming or Macroreading® through the manageable chunk you have chosen, to pick up the gist of what it's about.

Then, demonstrate to yourself how it's possible to pick up the gist of a section through previewing by verbalising a brief summary of your section for 30 seconds or more. Do this either out loud to yourself or to someone you know.

Step 2 | Notes outline using key headings | 30 seconds – 2 minutes

Make an outline for your notes or memory map, dividing your page into segments, each with a heading, and leaving space to add the detail later (Step 6). Keep your headings short; key words or short phrases only.

It's fun to see what you can do from memory, but you can also add headings open-book.

Step 3 | Read for understanding | 3 – 5 minutes

Read your manageable chunk for good understanding, to acquire and absorb the information. For any important keyword or key idea that sums up what the sentence or paragraph is about place a tick in the margin next to the line you are reading, or highlight the key word.

You may end up with three or four consecutive lines with ticks – that's ok. Prioritise. It can't all be truly important.

Remember the 80/20 rule. 80% of the ideas come from around 20% of the words.

Step 4 | Reread a little faster | 2.5 – 4.5 minutes

Reread to check you've got everything truly important.

Notice anything ticked or highlighted, then confirm – is it truly important? If yes, double or triple tick. If no, that's fine. Move on.

---

* This method assumes you are working with hard copy, i.e. printed material on paper. That way you can identify beginning and end points with a pencil tick or paper clips or sticky notes and tick important points in the margin.
If material to be remembered is a .pdf or can be read online, you can adapt this method by highlighting or marking up a document electronically.

Is there anything truly important not yet ticked? Go ahead and tick or highlight, creating a double or triple tick.

As you've already read this material, speed up your reading rate just a little. Use your finger, hand, pen, pencil or highlighter to guide your eyes as you read.

Step 5 | Postview | 30 seconds – 1 minute

Spend around 30 to 60 seconds performing a postview, scanning only those lines you have ticked or highlighted as important. You are reading only the important parts of the manageable chunk of information. This is your final 'cram' before starting to make your notes from immediate recall.

Step 6 | Start notes – first from memory | 1–4 minutes

As soon as you have finished the postview, cover your reading material and add to your notes whatever you can immediately recall. Use the headings in your outline as memory triggers for the detail you are adding.

Step 7 | Add notes – open-book*, use another colour | 1–5 minutes

When your notes are complete with as much as you can retrieve from memory, only then open your reading material again. Go through your text and cross-reference, that is, check whatever you ticked or highlighted is included in your notes. If not, add it in, using another colour.

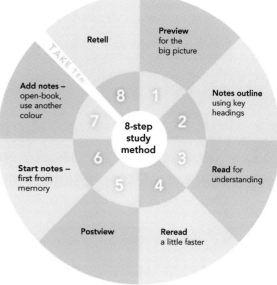

Take ten | 10 minutes

Then take a ten-minute break.

Step 8 | Retell | 1–5 minutes

After your ten-minute break (no longer), verbalise what you can remember out loud to yourself or to someone you know.

Review again after 48 hours, then 7 days, after you first studied the material.

Finally...

You will blitz your exams!

---

* When referring to 'open-book' it means with printed material open. Your information may not necessarily be in 'book' form.

Letter to the reader

DO YOU

- **Find study boring?**
- **Get drowsy while studying?**
- **Find it hard to focus and pay attention?**

If you said 'yes', this book shows you how to learn so you remember **more** for **longer**.

Based on the science of how your brain works, the eight step method described in *Brainpower Smart Study* is easy and effective. For the first time, you'll have a fail-safe way to encode information into your memory.

Most students simply read and make notes. Apart from a quick review of these notes leading up to a test, they just hope for the best. Only at the moment of truth – the examination – do they realise what they **don't** know.

This is what I did at high school and first year university, with mediocre marks. Then I found a better way, and started getting superior results.

Since that time I poured my heart and soul into learning everything I could about memory improvement and how to study. I read every book on the subject and lived and breathed it.

As a result of being immersed in it for over two decades I'm now considered an expert in this field, so I'm well qualified to help you.

Imagine finding out what you don't know at the time of learning, rather than the exam. Once you know what you don't know, you can assign time to master it. This brings major improvement to your study efficiency and outcomes.

This book details an 8-step study method (until now available only via instructor-led workshops). By changing how you study, you'll change your life!

You'll be amazed how easily you learn and achieve better test results. Your grades will soar. Your fellow students will be impressed. Life will offer you better choices. Doors once closed will open.

Some methods used by students take more work than is necessary. For example, the top student of a Sydney high school told me he would record himself reading aloud the information to be learned, then listen to it over and over. I asked him how many times he listened to these recordings. His answer?

Up to 50 times each recording, leading up to final exams. This is a repetition tactic, and oh so time-consuming.

Another high-achieving graduate I talked with told me her favourite tactic was to cover up her notes and ask herself questions about what was in her notes. For example, if she was learning about problems in developing countries, she'd conceal her notes on that topic and turn it into a question: 'What problems face developing countries?' This is a much easier and more efficient method of studying.

But successful study needs more than a few study tips, it needs a total learning process. In this book, you are going to learn an 8-step method that keeps your mind alert while learning. It's ideal for solo study of factual material.

And here's the good news: a short break after a period of total focus is an essential part of the process.

By learning how to learn using this 8-step method you'll remember more for longer, leading to better grades and exam results. How does that sound?

Once your brain knows what's expected of it, it works for you in exciting new ways that will simply amaze you.

How to use this book

This is a practical book. The best way to use it is:

1. First read the whole book so you understand how and why the method works.

2. Then apply each step with your study material, using the 8-step wheel diagram – Standard or Advanced version – as a reference.

Introduction

WHEN I WAS RE-DESIGNING OUR how-to-study workshop, I went to the local library and borrowed a major text by the distinguished Cambridge University psychologist, Alan Baddeley: *The Psychology of Memory*. As I read, I held this question in mind: 'What's the one thing people studying for exams, or learning any information, need to know about how memory works, which influences how they should study?'

Finally, I found this piece of gold, '**Recall of an item tends to increase its probability of subsequent recall.**[1]

That's it! When we are learning anything, we are more likely to remember what we have already remembered through testing, because testing makes us recall the information, which creates the neural pathway in the brain for subsequent recall. Recalling information trains the brain cells to recall the information more easily next time. And what was one thing absent from my study method when I was a student? Self-testing!

Here's the key. When students build into their study method more self-testing opportunities, they have better recall, better memory. This is known as the Testing Effect.[2]

How lightning works

Researchers asked 282 university students to watch a computer animation about how lightning works.[3]

Some students watched the video a second time, others were asked to write from memory a short description of how lightning works.

When tested one week later, the students who practised retrieving the information by writing their own explanation from memory did better than the group who watched the animation a second time.

What does this result mean for anyone who is studying?

If when you study you merely read and make notes then reread either the text or your notes, it's like watching the animation a second time.

If when you study you read then write notes from memory, it's like the group who were asked to write from memory a short description of how lightning works.

If you want to remember something, explain it from memory. Test yourself.

The Testing Effect: the missing link

The Testing Effect is the missing link in most people's study process. How-to-study methods have virtually ignored self-testing as a technique to improve learning. However, many successful students use self-testing during learning, like the high-achieving graduate who liked to cover up her notes then quiz herself about the topic.

In the SQ3R study method[4] from 1970 – Survey – Question – Read – Recite – Review – the Question step is a form of self-testing. After surveying, you are meant to spend 30 seconds thinking about what you just scanned; asking yourself what do you know.

But one problem with the 'Question' step is that to question is a purely mental activity. Most people just won't do it. Stop and question yourself about what you just previewed? That is an abstract activity, invisible, and easy to skip.

Most of us are only human. It's easier to move on quickly to the next tangible step, to read. It requires discipline and patience to stop and think.

Instead, in the eight steps the self-test is active. Step 6 is 'Start notes – first from memory': write down what you can remember after reading.

What's an easy, tangible, active way to test yourself? Answer: start making your notes immediately after reading, from memory.

Study tips vs. a total study method

Most 'how-to-study' information gives good study tips that on their own are useful, such as: don't watch TV or do stuff online at the same time as studying; review your day's lecture notes again at night before sleep; and so on.

But there are not many complete step-by-step study procedures for students to follow. This book describes a total study method of eight easy-to-follow steps.

The procedure is proven and based on our pioneering work in speed reading and study skills.

Until now, this information was available only through our live workshops and multimedia. Now, in this book you'll discover a step-by-step process.

It's easy, it works if you apply all eight steps, and it's a study method based on evidence-based neuroscience and how the brain works.

An overview of the 8-step study method

The eight steps deconstruct the task to 'read and make notes' into a series of smaller, separate steps. It's based on how your brain works, so you'll remember the material better.

Let me reassure you, you still end up with detailed notes of the text to use for later review. But you'll construct these notes bit by bit, much like adding pieces to a jigsaw.

In a sequence of steps you'll build a bigger, detailed picture. And by doing it this way, you'll learn the material more thoroughly the first time you study it, and recall it better when you need to.

Instead of simply reading the text once and constructing detailed notes open-book as you go, you:

1 – **Preview** for the big picture

2 – **Notes outline** using key headings

3 – **Read** for understanding

4 – **Reread** a little faster

5 – **Postview**

6 – **Start notes** – first from memory

7 – **Add notes** – open-book, use another colour

   Take ten

8 – **Retell**

Then review regularly following the 10 / 48 / 7 rule explained in Chapter 10.

Stay relaxed

In the pages that follow each step is explained in detail. So relax and read on. It will become clear.

Getting started

Reading on paper or on screen

ONE OF THE KEYS IS MARKING the text you are learning with a pencil, pen or highlight pen. The easiest way to do this is to work with reading material on paper.

Research shows that reading speed on a computer is around 20% - 30% slower than reading from paper.[1] This is another reason to work with paper-based text. But if you have a digital pen using digital ink to mark a document or add marginalia online as you read, that's fine.

Study materials

You will need:

- the reading material to study – a copy you can mark with pencil and/or highlight pens (it could be the original, or a photocopy)

- two paper clips

- pencil or highlighter

- set of coloured pens

- notepad

- watch, clock or some way to keep track of time.

Studying the old way, you might have opened your text and just started reading or making notes. Studying this way, start by first choosing the chunk of material to study.

Your goal is to walk away master of this specific section of the text. You'll be amazed to find you have superior memory of this particular chunk of information. As you study one chunk at a time with total focus and no other distractions you'll have superior recall of everything you choose to study this way. You'll accurately remember more for longer.

Manageable chunks

You may have heard the saying 'Don't bite off more than you can chew'. Your first decision is how much to study in one study session. You need to decide on the length of the section to 'bite off' and ensure it is a **manageable** chunk of information.

A manageable chunk is the amount that can be studied and remembered in one sitting, one learning session. It might be seven pages, a couple of pages, one page or even half a page.

What you're looking for is an amount that will turn into one-page-worth of notes, i.e. you estimate that when you construct your notes, summarising that section, they would fill up no more than one page.

(Density of ideas)*

The length of a section to study each time depends on the density of the ideas in the text.

If a chapter is 20 pages, perhaps five of those 20 pages might be one manageable chunk. If the text is quite detailed, with lots of headings or words in bold, one page (instead of five) might be a manageable chunk.

Compare these two paragraphs:

Paragraph 1

A brain cell is called a neuron. Neurons do not touch each other directly, but are in close proximity. Brain cells communicate with each other through an electrochemical process. Signals travel between neurons across the connection gap called a synapse. Did you know in the nervous system there are more than 10^{15} (10 to the 15th power) synaptic connections? That's one thousand times one trillion, which is 1, followed by 15 zeros, or 1,000,000,000,000,000.

Paragraph 2

Brain cells communicate by passing signals from one cell to another. A chemical carries the message and this chemical must cross a small space between each cell to be successful. There are more than 1,000,000,000,000,000 (1 followed by 15 zeros) brain cell connections.

Paragraph 2 is a simple description of easy to medium level difficulty. Paragraph 1 contains more scientific terms, has a lot of information and is more 'dense'.

How much detail is there in your section?

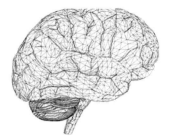

About the brain

How many bytes of information can the brain store?

The memory capacity of the brain is around three terabytes.

Just over one thousand megabytes equals one gigabyte, and just over one million megabytes equals a terabyte.

1,024 megabytes = 1 gigabyte
1,024 gigabytes = 1 terabyte
1,048,576 megabytes = 1 terabyte

• • •

How many synapses in the brain?

If you counted one synapse per second, you'd count for 32 million years.[2]

---

*There are some paragraphs that are optional to read. These are sections you can easily skip without losing the key ideas. The headings of these optional paragraphs are marked with brackets. Read or skip, it's your decision.

How many headings?

Notice whether the text is formatted as words only, or whether it includes headings which serve as signposts to the reader.

Choose your chunk

Select a section that corresponds to what you estimate might fit on one page when you do your notes summary. You will jot down probably no more than six headings on any one page in your notes.

If your section might require 12 headings or two pages of notes, the section you've chosen is too long.

Mark the beginning and end of your section with two paper clips.

As you read about all eight steps of the method you'll discover why you are selecting one-page-worth-of-notes of reading material. It means you'll bite off only as much as you can chew; only as much as you can digest in one sitting.

Chapter Summary

Mark beginning and end

Estimate one manageable chunk of material to study. Don't select too big a chunk. Mark the beginning and end of your section to study with two paper clips.

CHAPTER 1

BIG PICTURE

Preview your manageable chunk of information and if you can, then do a verbal summary.

TAKE YOUR MANAGEABLE CHUNK of text to study and look first at the big picture by starting with an overview. The goal is simply to gain a general idea of the content, the gist of it. Relax as you preview reading material. You can't expect to fully understand it at preview stage. You'll be reading for understanding in step 3.

Aid to understanding

Previewing is not only an aid to memory, it's an aid to understanding. Have you ever watched a movie a second time and noticed things that escaped your attention on first viewing? When the goal of reading is to remember, previewing before reading is beneficial.

It is good practice to start wide, gain a global view first, and then go deep to focus on the detail.

> **Have you ever watched a movie a second time and noticed things that escaped your attention on first viewing?**

Easy way to start

Do you ever find it difficult to open your textbook to even begin to study? A preview is less demanding and eases you effortlessly into action.

How fast is a preview?

A comfortable preview rate varies from person to person. For most people, twice as fast as their comfortable reading-for-understanding rate is about right.

An average reader reads around 200–300 words per minute. Their preview rate might be around 400–600 words per minute – twice as fast as their usual reading rate. If a typical paperback has around 300 words per page, then it might take around 30 seconds to preview a page.

For a speed reader who reads above 1000 words per minute (and that's with good understanding or it's not speed reading), their preview rate might be 2000 words per minute or around 11 seconds per page.

Preview techniques

Skim reading can be a useful preview technique. Skim reading means picking out key words as clues to understanding. Let your eye 'skim' over the lines, jumping from keyword to keyword.

> ... a method of previewing we call Macroreading®. It's similar to skimming, but more systematic and strategic.

Macroreading®

In our Speed Reading classes we teach a method of previewing we call Macroreading[1]. It's similar to skimming, but more systematic and strategic.

Macroreading is scanning the text with a relaxed eye focus at a rate around twice as fast as a comfortable reading rate, to gain an overview.

To Macroread, tell your eyes to slightly defocus, then move your finger, hand or a pen as a visual aid in a zigzag or 's' motion down the page, scanning all the words for the gist, or whatever you can pick up.

ZIGZAG

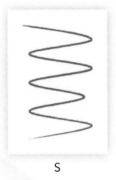

S

If your eyes are jumping from keyword to keyword, that's skimming, not Macroreading, but either method is fine to use to preview.

So far...

You've already:

- decided on the length of the section you are to study
- marked beginning and end points with two paperclips.

And you are about to:

- preview, using your finger, hand or pen as a visual pacer to guide your eyes, using a zigzag or 's' hand motion.

 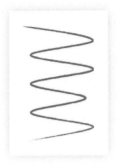

(What is 'proper' reading?)

Remember, in previewing, you are not reading for detail. Just allow your eyes to scan over the section you've selected, getting a feel for the big picture by noticing keywords or picking up the gist.

I don't agree with the opinion, 'If you don't read it *properly* you may as well not read it at all'.

What is 'proper' reading anyway?

You might ask yourself: 'Isn't it a waste of time scanning words this way? How is it possible to read and understand at twice as fast as my comfortable reading rate?'

Well, here's the secret: skilled readers don't read at a single rate. They match their reading rate to their purpose.

In my experience as a Speed Reading instructor, I've observed many CEOs and Senior Managers use skim reading and Macroreading as a way to get through their 'must reads'. If all you need is an overview of a text, then previewing **is** proper reading.

I certainly don't read everything at one single base rate. As a skilled reader, I have a range of rates. I match my reading rate to my purpose. I can choose to speed up and scan when all I want to extract is an overview. I can slow down to a comfortable pace to read for understanding.

Become a skilled reader; learn to read with a variable reading rate depending on your purpose.

Chapter Summary

Preview
Quickly preview your manageable chunk by skim reading or Macroreading® to get an overview of what it's about.

► CHAPTER 2
RECALL OUTLINE

Use visual design elements and subheadings to set up a rough outline for your notes.

NOW THAT YOU'VE GOT A BIG PICTURE of your material, and **before** you read for understanding, prepare an outline for your notes. This outline or skeleton consists of headings only, to act as triggers for your recall. You add detail to this outline later, after you read the text for understanding.

This step encourages you to interact with the material, to make connections, and to see relationships between ideas. By interacting with the material using the eight steps your mind stays active, thinking about the text. This is known as critical thinking. As you move from big picture to detail, you see how ideas connect. You'll remember more for longer and become master of the topic.

Headings and sub-headings

As you previewed your section, did you encounter headings and sub-headings in the text? That's often the case with textbooks and study material. If headings are provided, your task is easy. These headings probably form your notes outline.

If there are no headings, use your power of critical thinking to devise your own sub-headings to summarise the content. Creating your own sub-headings gets easier with practice.

If you divide your page into segments (read more about this in the paragraph on visual design elements later in this chapter) you can assign one segment of the page to each sub-heading, up to six and no more than nine.

Research by George Miller published as 'The Magical Number Seven, Plus or Minus Two'[1] makes us aware that seven is the average number of items a person can remember at one time.

So keeping your study chunk to seven sub-headings or less makes it possible for your brain to memorise it all in one sitting. As long as we learn in manageable chunks and take frequent short breaks, we can continuously add to memories our brain stores.

(Make non-traditional notes)

Traditional notes are usually linear in design and process i.e. words are added left to right, one word at a time, one line at a time, down the page. But your brain doesn't think in a linear way; neural pathways form networks and encode information in images as well as words.

Chapter 13 describes how to construct memory maps, a diagramming technique for notes using branches, keywords and colour. For now, just distribute your ideas around the page, shifting from a traditional linear structure to notes that are global, i.e. a whole page at a time, and more visual.

It's okay to do this open-book, cross referencing with your reading material.

Go freehand

I don't know if you are in the habit of typing your notes using a computer, but I'm going to suggest you do your notes:

- with pen and paper, especially using a variety of coloured pens
- freehand on unruled pages
- unplugged, i.e. no computer, no hardware, no software

Firstly, typing promotes a traditional linear approach. Freehand pen and paper allows you to distribute your ideas around the page, rather than line by line. You use the geography of the page – the north, south, east and west.

It's often better to use unruled paper for your notes. Because we are using the geography of the page, ruled lines are unnecessary.

Secondly, in the exam will you be writing by hand or typing? Unless you are allowed to take in your laptop, practice writing by hand. Some examiners may even judge you on the legibility of your handwriting.

... distribute your ideas around the page, rather than line by line

Coloured pens

There are good reasons to use various coloured pens for notes, which is discussed in Chapter 7.

Always use at least two contrasting colours, for example:

- blue and red
- black and brown
- pencil and pen.

Choose a pen colour that is easy to read (don't pick a yellow pen to write up your notes) and shades you can tell apart easily.

Visual design elements

Before adding sub-headings open-book,
spilt up your page by dividing it into six sections,
one for each sub-heading. It might look like this:

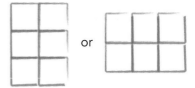

You can experiment drawing different shapes e.g.

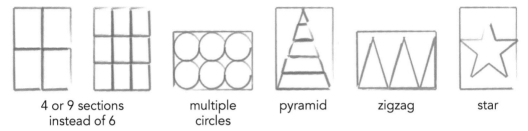

| 4 or 9 sections instead of 6 | multiple circles | pyramid | zigzag | star |

Treating your page of notes as a whole page and adding visual design elements aids memory by association. In fact it's good if you make the design of each page of notes slightly different. The novelty of various shapes is an aid to recall.

(Portrait vs. landscape)

Which way to orient your notes? Traditional notes are usually on 'portrait' orientation, where the height of the page is greater than the width, because it's easier to read shorter lines of text. A 'landscape' orientation, where the height of the page is less than the width, often suits a more visual approach to note-taking.

portrait   landscape

It's your decision whether you work with your notepad in portrait or landscape orientation. Personally, I prefer landscape. But I suggest you try both ways to decide which you prefer.

Chapter Summary

Notes outline

Start your notes by making an outline, open-book, referring to your reading material.

Copy headings to your outline. (If headings not provided, devise your own.)

Create headings within a visual structure, leaving space to add the detail later (step 6).

Tip: Keep headings short: use key words or short phrases.

CHAPTER 3

ABSORB

Read for understanding, ticking in the margin important points or highlighting keywords as you go. This is called active reading.

WE'VE ALREADY COMPLETED TWO STEPS of the eight before reading for understanding.

1. We've previewed to gain the **big picture**, to become familiar with what's to come and to identify main headings or key points. The preview is like reading a map prior to travelling the territory.

2. We've created an **outline**, adding headings onto a page in our notepad and leaving space to add detail later.

These steps have prepared our minds for the next step: to read for understanding, to **absorb** the information.

Active reading and critical thinking

As you read, you are going to mark important points in the margin with a pencil tick or highlight keywords. Identifying key points while reading keeps you mentally alert and cultivates active rather than passive reading. Passive reading is simply reading for understanding. Locating target information while reading is an active process requiring you to use your powers of critical thinking.

The brain doesn't remember sentences word for word. It remembers ideas. When you identify a key word or key point, you are focusing on the essential ideas of the text. As you later recall those key ideas, they trigger your memory of the words surrounding those key points, giving it meaning. This is what's called the context, the words surrounding the key ideas, explaining them.

Truly important vs. important

When studying a text for the first time, your target information is most likely anything 'truly important'. Notice I wrote 'truly' important.

A paragraph contains both key ideas and context – the words explaining those key ideas, giving them meaning.

Marking the text as you read aids memory by identifying the most important bits to remember, rather than trying to remember it all. You can trust your brain, knowing that focusing on key ideas automatically triggers your memory of the rest of the information.

Marking the text identifies the important points you'll soon be adding to your notes. But here's the trick. The 8-step method includes a reread, which means you get to identify the 'truly' important during the second read, with the benefit of hindsight.

Have you ever been studying, and as you continued reading through the text, realised a section you initially considered important actually was not?

Critical thinking skill

Identifying what's important as you read is an advanced critical thinking skill worth cultivating. There's power in being able to identify the essence of a paragraph.

Exercise

Do this exercise. Identify the key ideas from this paragraph about fitness by circling the key words (circle no more than two consecutive words).

> **Physical fitness increases the efficiency of your lungs and your heart. It helps you control your weight and is an aid in controlling tension and anxiety. It also helps you withstand physical fatigue for a longer time.**

You'll find our example at the end of this chapter.

Tick or highlight

Select either a pencil (so you can erase markings later) or fluorescent marker. With pencil or highlighter in hand, identify the important points as you read.

Pencil ticks in margin

Read with a pencil in hand and place a tick in the margin against every line containing a key point.

Right or left margin, it doesn't matter. I tend to use the outside margins (left hand side of the left page, right hand side of the right page).

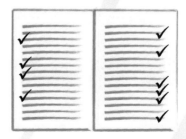

Highlighting key words

If using a fluorescent marker, highlight only key points. Please aim to limit yourself to maximum two consecutive words.

The purpose of highlighting is to identify the essence of the text.

Have you ever picked up a book where someone has marked whole paragraphs? There's no way of telling apart what's truly important from supporting detail. Use a highlighter sparingly and avoid marking up a whole sentence or paragraph.

An exception might be a definition or quotable quote. Highlight only the truly important words so it's easy for your brain to digest and remember.

Less is more

Here's the paradox: less is more. The fewer words you highlight the more you remember.

The more you distil the information down to the essential, the easier it is to remember. Your brain remembers key points better than sentences.

Research study

A research study[1] contrasted the lecture notes of high-achieving students with the notes of low-achieving students. One of these two groups of students' notes had fewer words on the page. Can you guess which group, the high or low achievers?

The correct answer is, the high-achievers, because these students did two smart things.

1. They actively listened during lectures to identify key points.
2. They wrote down mostly only key points to trigger their memory.

Low-achieving students did the exact opposite. They wrote copious notes. In fact, their notes were more like dictation. Writing notes word-for-word fosters passive listening. These students actually remembered less because they were concentrating on writing rather than active listening and critical thinking. They were working hard rather than smart.

Writing keywords as trigger words is more effective than writing copious notes.

Other marginalia

There are more ways to mark up text beyond simple ticks or highlighting. Develop your own repertoire of symbols or personal codes to add in the margin (called marginalia), for example:

- **Underlining or circling** a key word or phrase (remember to restrict yourself to what's truly important.)

- **Three asterisks or other symbol** – use this very occasionally to make truly important ideas stand out

- **Vertical line or bracket** to indicate 3 or 4 lines of high importance, where most of the words are important

- **Numbered points** – especially when there is a list of points but the author has not numbered them, or perhaps words like, 'firstly', 'secondly' are used

- **Question mark** or exclamation point

- **Arrows** to indicate relationships

- **Key words** – when there are no sub-headings supplied, create your own in the margin as an active reading task.[2]

(Feeling guilty about marking the book?)

I've observed in our how-to-study classes that some people avoid highlighting or making a pencil tick and just make a faint dot instead. Perhaps it's a library or borrowed book, or they intend selling the book after the course is finished.

Those are reasonable concerns. Borrowed items should be returned in good condition and there can be better resale value for books with fewer pen marks.

If that's the case use pencil rather than pen, so it's easy to erase later, or work with a photocopy.

But please remember why you are reading. Your first goal is to learn the content with the least effort. Other concerns, such as preserving the book for later resale, are secondary.

By the way, I encourage you to use your pencil as a visual pacer to guide your eyes as you read; it increases reading rate. Those who have done our Speed Reading course already know this trick.

(Create your own table of contents)

Many books have a few blank pages at the front and back. Why not take advantage of these pages to create your own table of contents? You can list the topics you regard as important and the page numbers next to them.

That way whenever you open that book you have a record of what you found to be truly important the last time you read it.

I now have a library of books marked up with a personal table of contents, with the topics most useful to me. Anytime I refer to this book again, rather than having to leaf through the book looking for all the marked-up sections, I can go straight to those topics and page numbers identified as truly important last time I read. This is a real time-saver.

Reading duration

Because you've selected a manageable chunk of information, you'll only need a few minutes to read it for understanding. How long you need for this reading depends on:

- your reading rate
- length of your section
- density of the text.

As a rough guide, in Step 3 you might read for as little as 2 minutes and for not much longer than 5 minutes. The reason for studying small chunks at a time becomes clear when we discuss Step 6 when you start your notes from immediate recall.

Here's possible durations for each of the eight steps:

Step 1 – Preview – 30 seconds – 1 minute

Step 2 – Outline – 30 seconds – 2 minutes

Step 3 – Read – 3 – 5 minutes

Step 4 – Reread – 2.5 – 4.5 minutes

Step 5 – Postview – 30 seconds – 1 minute

Step 6 – Start notes – 1–4 minutes

Step 7 – Add notes – 1–5 minutes

Take ten – 10 minutes

Step 8 – Retell – 1–5 minutes

These timings are flexible and may change each time.

(Reading rate)

An average reader reads 200–300 words per minute. A speed reader might read non-fiction material at 700–1000 words per minute or faster.

A typical paperback has around 300 words per page, more or less, depending on font size. A textbook might be larger than a paperback, but if it has graphs, charts and illustrations, the words per page may also be around 300.

If your manageable chunk of information is four pages, then the duration of your reading for understanding will be around 4 minutes for an average reader, 2 minutes or less for a speed reader.

Ticking or highlighting should be done quickly, so it doesn't slow you down while you read.

(Studying deep vs. wide)

You are studying deep rather than wide. By that I mean you will have viewed your chunk of information four times, in steps 1, 3, 4 and 5:

Step 1 – preview

Step 3 – read

Step 4 – reread

Step 5 – postview

There's power in multiple reading. That's where good understanding and good memory comes from.

Chapter Summary

Read for understanding

Read your manageable chunk to understand and absorb the information. For any important key word or key idea that sums up what the sentence or paragraph is about, place a quick tick in the margin next to the line you are reading, or highlight the key word.

You may occasionally have three or four consecutive lines with ticks – that's ok. But do prioritise. It can't all be truly important.

Remember the 80/20 rule: 80% of the ideas come from around 20% of the words.

Exercise in identifying key points from chapter 3.

Physical fitness increases the efficiency of your lungs and your heart. It helps you control your weight and is an aid in controlling tension and anxiety. It also helps you withstand physical fatigue for a longer time.

Now that you've identified the key points (circled) only these words go in your notes.

TIP: a word repeated often makes a good heading for dot points. For example, 'Controls' might make a good heading for 'weight', 'tension' and 'anxiety' as dot points.

Once you've extracted the key points, you can focus your attention on remembering those key points, instead of trying to remember everything.
You've distilled the information to its essence.

CHAPTER 4

IMPORTANCE CHECK

Reread a little faster to identify and mark the truly important points. Distil the information to its essence.

WHEN INFORMATION HAS TO BE COMMITTED to memory, reread to locate the truly important points.

This enables you to:

- confirm the information that has to be remembered
- identify, with the advantage of having seen it before, any important information that might otherwise have been missed.

Read the same section again to recognise what you previously identified as important. You can now prioritise the information which is truly important with a double or triple tick.

This is an active reading task, to search for truly important information, the essence of what it's about.

Idea gaps

You're actually rereading to locate idea gaps. The first read identified what you thought was important, based on a first view of the material.

Now that you are viewing it a second time, read asking yourself these two questions:

1. Is what I've ticked or highlighted truly important?
   (If what's already ticked isn't that important, that's no big deal. It can stay ticked.)
2. Is there anything truly important I've missed that's not yet ticked or highlighted?

There's always a chance, with the perspective of having read it once, you might locate an important point missed on the first read. If you find one, tick it.

Double and triple ticks

You can now introduce double and triple ticks. As you read, add double or triple ticks against the few items more important than the rest. This makes them stand out from the other important points you marked.

As you are reading you might think to yourself, 'That was such an important point, it's worthy of two extra ticks', making a triple tick.

(If highlighting, you might add an asterisk in the margin using the highlight pen.)

You'll end up with margins marked up with single, double and triple ticks. If you ticked or highlighted too much during the first read, you can leave these as single ticks or highlights.

You are constantly refining to locate the essential key points to trigger your memory. You are distilling the information down to its essence.

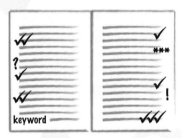

Reading faster

Remember in Chapter 1 we discussed using a range of reading rates, not reading everything at a single base rate?

Consider this. So far you've previewed and actively read your manageable chunk. The 'importance check' reread is actually your third view of the information. Do you think increased familiarity might enable you to read slightly faster?

Because it is your second reading, you may notice you automatically do read it faster

There are a couple of simple tricks to being able to read faster.

1. Warm up your brain with a preview prior to reading.
2. Use a visual pacer when you read to reduce the poor reading habits of fixation and sub-vocalisation (see the Glossary for a description of these habits).

The pencil or highlighter you are using to mark the text is perfect for this. Simply run it along the line under the words as you read to guide your eyes, or you can use your finger or hand instead. There's no need to run it along the whole line. If you prefer, simply the middle third of each line will do. Experiment with different ways until you settle on your preference.

If you find the pacer distracting at first, please persevere, as it really does help you read faster. It may take up to an hour of reading this way before you feel comfortable using a visual guide when you read. You will get used to it.

During the reread, confirm in your mind that you recognise whatever you ticked or highlighted. For example you might tell yourself:

- 'Yes, I remember seeing that.'

- 'Yes, I read that.'
- 'Yes, that was important.'

and so on.

You are reminding your brain of what you previously read. This aids your memory.

(What if I miss something?)

While doing the importance check, you can expect your reading rate to speed up slightly. It doesn't matter if you miss a bit. This is a subsequent read, an additional read.

Alternatively, you might be surprised how much your brain takes in at a rate 50% faster than your usual reading rate, especially when you've read it before.

Remember, the purpose of rereading to check importance is to:

1. help you prioritise the most important information from the least important
2. aid your memory.

Chapter Summary

Reread a little faster

Reread your manageable chunk as an importance check. As you've already read this material, speed up your reading rate just a little. Use your finger, hand, pencil or highlighter to guide your eyes as you read.

1. Notice anything you've ticked or highlighted. Confirm – is it truly important? If yes, double or triple tick. If no, that's fine. Move on.

2. Is there anything truly important not yet ticked? Go ahead and tick or highlight, creating a double or triple tick.

CHAPTER 5

NAIL IT

Postview the truly important information by reading only that which is ticked or highlighted. This is prior to adding to notes first from memory.

SIMILAR TO A PREVIEW, A POSTVIEW is viewing the material twice as fast as comfortable by skimming or Macroreading.

But during the postview you're not scanning or skimming the whole section as you did in the preview. You're reading just those lines with ticks or highlights.

Why do a postview?

The answer lies in understanding the next step.

Step 6 of the 8-step method is to add to notes **from immediate recall**. Immediately after this postview, add information to your recall outline, to form notes or a memory map. The postview is like a final cram before you test your memory.

Studying the old way, you might have written all your notes open-book, copying straight from your reading material. Studying the new way, after having previewed, read, reread, and postviewed your section, you write your notes from your immediate memory.

This means you self-test what you know, after having viewed the material four times.

Why do this? Let's consider memory and how it works.

Prompted vs. unprompted recall

There are two types of recall – prompted and unprompted.

Unprompted recall is when you search your memory to retrieve an item of information. For example, you might be asked a question and you search your memory for the answer. If you are successful and can retrieve the answer we would say you had unprompted recall of that item of information.

Example 1 – unprompted recall

Beijing is the capital of which Asian nation?

Answer: _____

Prompted recall is when you recognise the info only after it's mentioned or you see it written, perhaps as a list of options as in a multiple choice test.

Example 2 – prompted recall

Beijing is the capital of which Asian nation?
– Korea
– China
– Thailand

The second example is in the form of multiple-choice. The list of possible choices prompts or cues your recall. In the first example, you had to search your memory for the answer.

(Which is easier?)

Some multiple-choice tests, especially at university level, are so well designed it requires thorough knowledge of the topic to gain a pass mark. However, more often, multiple-choice is easier. When given a list of alternatives, it is usually easier to recognise the correct answer.

What you *don't* know

Remember the typical way most students study? *Read and make notes … reread notes … read and make notes … reread notes … read and make notes …*

With a method like that, you won't find out what you don't know til you get to the exam.

Don't you think it's better to find out what you don't know when you first learn it? Then you can spend extra time re-learning those bits until you are confident you know them too.

Reading when you know you'll self-test

Knowing that the next step is to add to your outline from immediate recall means you perform the postview with a heightened awareness of the content.

Through selective post-reading you focus on the important points, giving them your attention. You are deciding to remember. Your brain is primed, ready to be tested.

Chapter Summary

Action: Nail it with a quick postview

Spend around 30 to 60 seconds performing a postview: scanning only those lines you have ticked or highlighted as important. You are reading only the truly important points in your manageable chunk. This is your final cram before making your notes from your immediate memory.

CHAPTER 6

IMMEDIATE RECALL

Using the outline already created to trigger your memory, add to your notes first from memory.

> *An education isn't how much you have committed to memory, or even how much you know. It's being able to differentiate between what you do know and what you don't.*[1]
>
> *Anatole France*

WRITING DOWN WHAT YOU CAN remember after reading is called a 'memory dump'. This memory dump accesses the information you can remember using unprompted free recall.

Heading	Heading	Heading
Heading	Heading	Heading

How do you know you know something?

Writing notes from memory, prompted by your outline, tests and confirms what's stored in your memory.

Why is it important to test memory during study?

Research shows that successful recall of an item of information increases the likelihood of subsequent recall.[2]

Imagine the connections in your brain as like a road network with hundreds of thousands of roads. For an item of information to be retrieved, it has to travel a short way down one of these roads.

Every time a specific item of information is recalled, it travels down the same short road.

That's how memory works. The first time you retrieve a memory, it travels down a short road in your brain, the brain cell pathway. It becomes easier to travel down the same road each time it's recalled.

In nature, a well-trodden path is easier to walk than where there is no path at all.

After you've remembered something once, you are more likely to remember it again.

Retrieving information creates the neural pathway in the brain that you'll use in subsequent recall. Anything you have previously recalled is more easily remembered.

Self-testing is a way of recalling information, so it makes sense to build in self-testing during learning. You are practising the exact same skill you need in the exam – retrieving information.

So just remember to remember; remember to test whether you know it.

Let me remind you of the study[3] in which university students were either shown how lightning works a second time or asked to write a short description from memory. A week later, students who had tested their memory by explaining did better than the students who saw the information a second time.

Practising retrieving information is better than re-studying or rereading.

Chapter Summary

Start notes – first from memory

After performing the postview, straight away while the information is in your working memory, start your notes without referring to the text, i.e. closed-book, from memory. This tests your immediate recall.

Perhaps you are thinking, 'That sounds hard'.

And perhaps it is, but only at first. Let go, trust your brain will remember something, and add whatever comes to mind to your notes. Remember we've already set up a structure to your notes by creating an outline. This acts as a trigger for the detail you'll be adding.

If you come to a mental blank and feel you can't remember any more, don't give up, just keep trying a few moments longer. Often, after a temporary lull you'll get a second wind, and off you go again, adding to your notes.

Step 6 debrief

How did you go? How much information were you able to immediately recall from memory?

- Were you surprised by how much you could retrieve?
- Did you remember more than you thought you would?
- Once started, did you get into a flow, recording one idea after the other?

Or perhaps you recalled very little? If that's the case, let me reassure you, that's probably just because it's a new skill that you are doing for the first time. Relax. Once you get used to including this self-testing step in your study procedure after reading, information comes to you from memory in a flow.

Are you thinking right now, 'I don't want to have to start my notes first from memory. I'd rather just add the notes open-book.' Well, that's the temptation! It's easy to add to notes open-book. But it's not smart. Smart students know that if you want free recall in the exam, you need to use free recall while first learning that information. Doesn't that make sense?

Most students don't self-test as part of their learning method. Yet it's so easy and effective to add this step. Just because you might be tempted to skip this step doesn't mean you should! It's up to you to include step 6 when studying. Step 6 is the key to the success of the 8-steps.

(Not a quick fix)

Success in study is not measured by how much time you spend studying, but how effective the time you spend studying is. If you spend four hours studying yet can't be certain you know the material, how effective were those four hours?

The eight steps may take less time, the same time, or even more time than the way you used to study, but you are investing time to save time. You'll learn your topic properly the first time and not waste as much time relearning later.

Your grades will soar and your peers will be impressed.

CHAPTER 7

ADD

Check everything you ticked or highlighted as important is included in your notes from memory. If not, add using a different colour pen.

NOW THAT YOU'VE USED YOUR IMMEDIATE recall to make notes under the headings in your outline, you are ready to add to your notes whatever you missed. It's important to check you didn't miss anything you'd identified as truly important. Do this step open-book.

How to add open-book

Go through your text and cross-reference i.e. check that whatever you ticked or highlighted is included in your notes, and included correctly. If not, add it in or correct it, **using a contrasting colour pen**.

Everything you add to your notes in this step is in a contrasting colour. Your notes end up colour-coded – one colour for what you wrote from immediate recall; another colour for what you missed then added open-book.

Remember to use key words rather than full sentences. And it's ok to change the word order.

You'll probably need only a few minutes to go through your text adding to your notes in a contrasting colour anything identified as important that's not already in your notes.

Straight away, you'll end up with a clear picture of two things:

1. what you remembered easily, in one colour

2. what you missed, in another colour.

You may need to spend more time re-learning and re-testing the things you missed.

Heading	Heading	Heading

Heading	Heading	Heading

Why another colour?

If everything you remember is one colour in your notes, and everything you add open-book is a contrasting colour, you have colour-coded both what you know and what you don't know. It points out the gaps in your knowledge.

Just imagine. Your notes will now display both what you remembered easily, and what you had to look up.

You've identified what is 'available' to you through unprompted recall. Anything added open-book was 'not available' to you. You can revise in a more focused and productive way.

In the next chapter we'll discuss how much information you can absorb in any one study session.

Chapter Summary

Add notes – open-book, use another colour

Go through your text and cross-reference i.e. check whatever you ticked or highlighted is included in your notes. If not, add it in another colour.

► CHAPTER 8
TAKE TEN

It's good practice to take a short break after inputting information to allow your brain time to store the new information.

NOW FOR THE GOOD NEWS. Take ten. You can now reward yourself with a short break of 10 minutes.

By taking a short break you are giving your brain a chance to transfer the information from working memory to long-term memory. Your brain needs ten minutes to store the information, like packing boxes onto a shelf.

Attention span

There's a legend about General Patton[1], a leader in the US army during World War II, who was known to ask anyone he came across working at their desk, *'Tell me. How long have you been sitting here?'* If they admitted it was more than 30 minutes, Patton would reply, *'Well it's time you got up and walked around and refreshed that brain of yours!'*

Our brains think more clearly after a break.

Frequently I'm asked: 'How long should I study in one sitting?' There are two ways to answer this question. There is a maximum for the average person, then there is your personal optimum – what's best for you personally.

The amount of time the brain can stay absorbed performing mental tasks and learning is around fifty minutes, maximum.

For many people it's less than fifty. Forty minutes might be the duration to aim for any time you're studying, absorbing, reading, thinking or focusing on any mental task.

Conversely, there's a minimum amount of time to focus to be effective and that's probably around 20–25 minutes. Any less than that and you are not allowing your brain to settle down and focus.

The 10-minute break is so important, you actually remember more for longer if you take a short break after information input and before the next session of fresh input.

But don't get sidetracked. Perhaps your phone has a countdown timer function. Keep your eye on the time and resume after precisely ten minutes, no longer.

Research supports the benefit of a 10-minute break after information input, followed by a physical activity which has nothing to do with the information you are learning.[2] You need to give your brain time to store it.

Physical exercise

Any kind of movement circulates the blood which carries oxygen to the brain, refreshing and oxygenating it. And that makes it easier for your brain to learn new things. So during your break, get up and get moving. Physical activities enhance learning, helping your brain create memories.

Any form of physical exercise that you can do in ten minutes is ideal for a break, including but not limited to:

- a ball game e.g. shoot a basketball through a hoop, hit a tennis ball against a wall, play table tennis, etc.
- a household task – prepare a snack, wash dishes, tidy up, feed a pet, take out garbage, water plants.
- take your dog for a ten minute walk
- practice a musical instrument
- do something with your hands – make something, draw something, repair something
- a number-based game such as Sudoku
- a video game requiring hand-eye co-ordination

But keep it strict to ten minutes, no longer.

The final step 8 of the study method comes next, discuss from memory what you've studied; have a conversation.

Chapter Summary

Take ten
Take a 10-minute break after completing step 7.
Give your brain a rest from further input and let your brain store the information you've just studied.
Do something non-verbal and physical rather than verbal like texting.

CHAPTER 9

CONVERSATION

After a 10-minute break, summarise verbally what's just been studied; retell it.

HAVE YOU EVER READ SOMETHING and felt you understood it while you were reading it, but when it came time to explain it, there were gaps in your memory?

Simply reading and making notes does not guarantee you can retrieve that information in a test.

Earlier, we discussed the importance of making learning active rather than passive. We suggested looking for keywords and making non-linear notes to keep our brains active while studying.

Have you ever had a feeling of panic before a test? Has fear of a poor result ever overwhelmed you so you could not think clearly?

To self-test during learning means you'll go into an exam feeling confident that you know you know it. This confidence calms the nerves and lowers exam stress.

In the Smart Study 8-step method we self-test twice:

Step 6: make notes from **immediate memory**

Step 8: after a 10-minute break, summarise verbally what's just been studied; retell it.

As you self-test, you grow brain cell connections needed to remember that information.

And we recommend regular review too; that's explained in Chapter 10.

Retelling

It's not always possible to study with a partner, but you might be able to phone a friend to tell it back. You might say something like: 'I've been studying about < topic >. Please let me tell you about it. Telling you helps me to remember.'

A conversation is an easy way to self-test, because it allows you to find out what gaps there are in your memory of what you've just studied. You find out what you don't know.

If a study buddy is not around, do you have a dog or cat? Even if they don't understand what you're talking about, they often respond to the attention!

Or you can simply say it out loud to yourself.

What are the advantages of retelling after studying?

Telling back what you know is quick and simple to do. As long as you are speaking from memory, it's testing what you know. You can test yourself easily and often after reading and studying. Because you are focusing on recalling what you do know, it boosts your confidence. You'll feel good about yourself. You'll feel like you're making progress.

Your ability to recall after reading and studying improves with practice. I've seen many students experience a mental blank in their first attempts to verbalise their summary. But as it became a regular part of their study process, it became easier. It became the norm.

After self-quizzing, whatever you recall is subsequently better remembered, because you created – or reinforced – the pathway in the brain that you use again in later recall.

To identify what you know means you also diagnose what you don't know. When you find out what you don't know, you can devote extra time relearning it. **So retelling fulfils both a testing and a learning function.**

Retelling also helps you distinguish between the essential and non-essential information. Hopefully you focus on the truly important.

Don't be tempted to skip retelling. Decide to always include a self-testing conversation after a short break. The break is a mini-reward that's good for your brain, while telling back is essential memory training. It creates the brain cell connections for that item of information.

Remember this law of memory:

Recall of an item increases the likelihood of subsequent recall.[1]

You study so what you are learning is available to you, you can retrieve it. If you've recalled information in the low-stress situation of personal study, you are more likely to be able to recall it in the high-stress environment of an exam. If you've read and made notes about a subject but never recalled those particular items of information from memory, you may find the stress of an exam blocks your memory.

By verbalising what you've learnt you'll be rewarded with better knowledge of your topics, improved grades. You'll also have the peace of mind that comes from demonstrating to yourself that you know it, rather than hoping you know it just because you read it.

Research in support of retelling

There is strong research to support the idea that when readers talk about what they read, it enhances their understanding and memory.[2]

Active review

Active review is testing our memory as part of the learning process. The distinction between passive and active review is like the distinction between prompted and unprompted recall discussed in Chapter 5.

Merely confirming you know something is passive; testing whether you know something is active. Previewing, reading, postviewing, are all passive. Writing notes open-book is passive.

But creating notes from memory is active. Retelling is testing your memory and active.

Most students study then hope they know it. With active review, you know you know it.

PASSIVE	ACTIVE
reading	self-testing, retelling
input	output
notes open book	notes from memory
hope you know it	confident, you know you know it

Here are the 8 steps:

1 – **Preview** for the big picture

2 – **Notes outline** using key headings

3 – **Read** for understanding

4 – **Reread** a little faster

5 – **Postview**

6 – **Start notes** – first from memory

7 – **Add notes** – open-book, use another colour

Take ten

8 – **Retell**

Chapter Summary

Retell
After a 10-minute break (no longer) retell what you can remember out loud to yourself or to someone you know.

CHAPTER 10

REGULAR REVIEW

Use the 10 / 48 / 7 rule to review over time what you study.

MOST STUDENTS REVIEW THEIR NOTES more than once leading up to the main test or exam, and that's great. Regular review prevents forgetting. If you forget less, it follows, you remember more.

But what is the best timing for review that cultivates optimum memory? How fast do we forget things?

10 minutes / 48 hours / 7 days rule

An early pioneer in the experimental study of human memory was a German professor at the University of Berlin, Hermann Ebbinghaus. In 1885 he published[1] results of his experiments testing recall of three-letter nonsense words such as:

DAX   NIM   TAL   YAT   KOJ   MIV   BAF   TEZ   DAJ   BOT

Ebbinghaus measured his recall of lists of these nonsense words, tested at different time delays after learning, e.g. after one day, after two days, after seven days.

He worked out that within two days he'd forgotten half or even two-thirds of the words.

Curiously, he also discovered that what remains in memory after two days also remains after seven. Most forgetting occurs in the first 48 hours. Forgetting is fast at first, then becomes gradual.

Memory isn't just about retrieval of information – it is also about stopping the forgetting that naturally occurs. You can see in the graph below, which shows the curve of forgetting newly learnt information, that we forget information at an exponential rate in the first hour after learning.

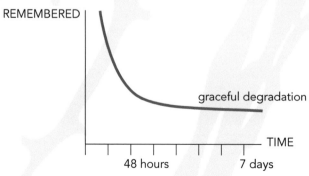

We can conclude from Ebbinghaus' research that it makes sense to space learning over several sessions rather than cram learning into one session.

It wasn't until 2005 that neuroscientist R Douglas Fields pinpointed 10 minutes as the ideal break after information input and before information recall.[2]

Memory maintenance – 10 / 48 / 7 rule

So, what can we do to stop the forgetting? Well, one thing is to understand that it's a matter of developing and maintaining memories rather than trying to 'fix' a broken memory.

Smart students review lecture notes the same night of a lecture, before sleep. Low-achieving students put away lecture notes until just before the exam. The smartest students review at least twice more after learning – at the two-day mark and at the seven-day mark.

Here's how to apply the 10 / 48 / 7 rule:

- Date your notes.

- Use the 8-step study method, which concludes with step 8: review what was just studied after a short break of **10 minutes**.

- Review again **48 hours** and then **7 days** after the original learning.

- Review today what you studied **48 hours ago** and **7 days ago.**

This diagram below represents, if studying daily,

- on day 3 review what you studied on day 1

- on day 4 review what you studied on day 2

- on day 5 review what you studied on day 3 and so on, until

- on day 8, review what you studied on day 6 and on day 1

- on day 9, review what you studied on day 7 and on day 2, and so on.

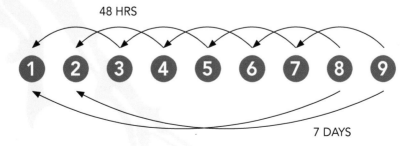

(Original learning)

Ebbinghaus discovered another principle: the time of original learning is the most important.

It's harder to re-learn information you've forgotten than to learn it correctly the first time.

Have you ever met somebody for the first time and for some reason got the name wrong? Instead of hearing Judy, you misheard it as Ruby? Have you noticed you constantly call them by that wrong name, even though you keep reminding yourself of the correct name?

It's harder to scour out wrong information to replace it with the correct new information. The time of original learning is the most potent.

This means it makes sense to study thoroughly during the initial learning session then follow up with regular review in the ideal spacing of: 10 minutes; 48 hours and 7 days. Do it right the first time.

Chapter Summary

10 / 48 / 7
Review your notes 10 minutes after study, then after 48 hours, then 7 days.

CHAPTER 11

MULTI-TASKING VS. MONO-TASKING

In this chapter find out how important it is to focus on one thing at a time; to resist the temptation to have your computer open keeping one eye on things happening online.

WHAT IS BETTER WHEN INPUTTING information to remember – multi-tasking or mono-tasking? Multi-tasking is doing two or more tasks at the same time. Focusing on one task at a time is mono-tasking.

What are some possible ways someone might multi-task while studying?

- updating their status online
- keeping up to date with everyone else's status online
- chatting online
- searching the web
- downloading music or videos
- adding a comment
- listening or singing along to music

Is it possible to spend lots of time studying yet not be effective? If one student decides to study 20 hours per week and another 10 hours, who will do better?

If the student studying 10 hours per week does so with computer off, with focused attention, might they gain better results than the student studying twice as long but with computer open, distracted with updating, downloading, chatting, monitoring or web searching?

One way to think about this – have you ever played the card game, Concentration? At the start, all cards are face down. Each player in turn reveals two cards. The goal is to locate matching pairs e.g. two queens, two fives. The player ending up with the most matching pairs wins.

To win, a player must have more than luck to flip over two cards of the same value. The smart player devises a strategy to memorise the location of cards that have been viewed.

A student who multi-tasks while studying – downloading, uploading, viewing, monitoring news feeds – is relying on luck to perhaps remember some of what they're studying.

The smart student closes their laptop and gives total focus to the process of inputting information to be remembered. Learning to focus during study and to eliminate distractions is probably the most important skill of all.

A goal of study time is to remember information. If the quality of your recall is evidence you spent your study time effectively, then test whether studying as a mono-task is more effective than multi-tasking while studying. You be the judge of what's more effective.

If resisting the temptation to do other things while studying gives you better results, then keep your laptop closed.

CHAPTER 12

MNEMONICS

Try creating your own mnemonics as memory triggers.

MNEMONICS ARE POEMS, SENTENCES, phrases or words to trigger your memory. Although spelling of the word 'mnemonic' begins with 'm', when saying the word the 'm' is silent. The word is pronounced 'neh-mon-ik'. In Greek myth the character of Mneme was the muse of memory.

Are you aware of the following mnemonic rhyme to help remember the number of days in a month?

> *Thirty days has September,*
> *April, June and November …*

Many people use this to help them identify whether a month has 30 days or 31.

The order of colours of the rainbow can be triggered with *Mr Roy G Biv,* standing for red, orange, yellow, green, blue, indigo, violet.

If you study music, you may come across this mnemonic for the notes of the musical scale: *Every Good Boy Deserves Fruit.*

There are mnemonics in first-aid. Someone tore a muscle at tennis and RICE was suggested: *Rest, Ice, Compression, Elevation.*

Scuba divers, to know which way to open and close oxygen tanks, use this mnemonic rhyme: *righty tighty, lefty loosey.*

If you were studying astronomy, you might remember the order of the planets in our solar system:

> Mercury
> Venus
> Earth
> Mars
> Jupiter
> Saturn
> Uranus
> Neptune
> Pluto[1]

by taking the first letter of each word to create a sentence, such as:

My very easy memory jingle seems useful naming planets.

Memory hooks

Vivid images associated with the information you want to remember are known as memory hooks.

It's okay to make up mnemonics that are fun, silly or slightly bizarre. In fact, it's a good thing! A sense of absurdity makes it vivid. And that makes it a good hook for your memory.

Create your own mnemonic

If you were studying Biology you might have to memorise the eight major categories used to rank organisms, from the largest grouping to the smallest:

Domain

Kingdom

Phylum

Class

Order

Family

Genus

Species

To invent a mnemonic to remember the order, write down the first letter of each word to be remembered, then create a sentence using only those letters in that order:

D_____ k_____ p_____ c_____ o_____ f_____ g_____ s_____.

For example

Do koalas prefer chocolate or fruit, generally speaking?

or

Dancing kangaroos play contentedly observing farmers growing seedlings.

or

Invent your own:

D_____ k_____ p_____ c_____ o_____ f_____ g_____ s_____.

► CHAPTER 13
MEMORY MAPPING FOR NOTES

Some people prefer memory maps over notes as a way to diagram information to make it more memorable.

A MEMORY MAP IS A DIAGRAMMING technique for notes using **branches** and **keywords** radiating from a **central** idea.

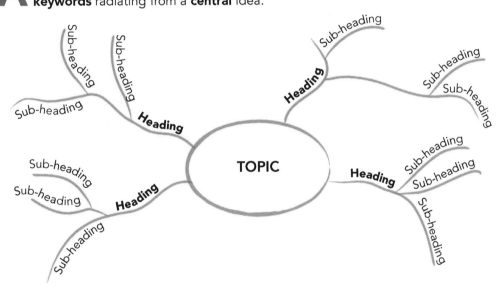

Memory maps are used in learning, brainstorming, memorising, visual thinking and problem-solving by students, educators, project managers, engineers, psychologists and many other professions.

You'll get superior results if you create your notes using memory mapping when studying.

(A memory map by any other name)

In research and literature you'll come across various other terms for them:

- concept map
- learning diagram
- recall pattern

BRAINPOWER SMART STUDY   43

- Tony Buzan's Mind Map®[1]
- knowledge map
- Cause and Effect diagram, Ishikawa diagram, Fishbone diagram
- tree diagram.

Memory maps have been around for a long time. An early example was developed by Porphyry of Tyros, a Greek thinker of the 3rd century AD who diagrammed concepts by Aristotle, a Greek philosopher from the 4th century BC.

Peter Ramus, a 16th century French philosopher, invented the flowchart diagram to describe the life of Cicero, an ancient Roman politician, lawyer, orator and philosopher.

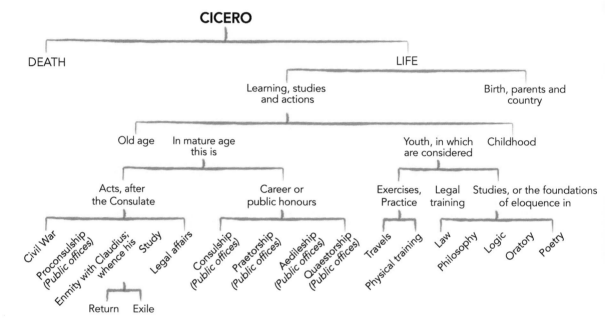

A flowchart can be considered a type of memory map.

In 1952, to help thought processes, Professor Ishikawa in Japan invented the Cause and Effect or Fishbone diagram as part of Total Quality processes.[2]

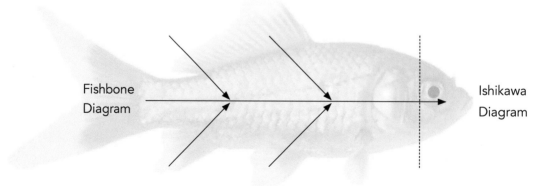

In recent years, there's been a growing trend to use memory maps for learning and in the workplace.

We use the term 'memory map' because:

- 'map' suggests we are using the north, south, east and west of the page
- 'memory' reminds us that, whichever type we use, it's an aid to better memory of the subject matter.

What does a memory map look like?

Let's look at what a memory map for taking notes might look like. We'll use the example of the children's tale, 'The three little pigs'.[3]

1. Start from the centre

The first rule of notes mapping is to start with a central line running almost to the edge of the page, (but not quite).

Your centre line can be in any direction: diagonal or vertical, straight or curved.

 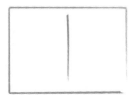 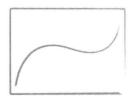

On this line write the main topic. Here are four possible versions:

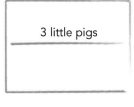 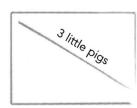

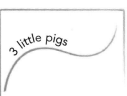 

2. Branches

Draw 4–6 branches. These lines can be straight or curved. Some people like to use a ruler, but I prefer freehand.

 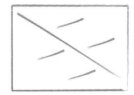 

3. Keywords

Use keywords or short phrases, no full sentences. You can even draw images or icons, if that works for you.

Who? What? Where? When? Why? How?

A useful method of focusing on what's important in a story is to ask yourself these six questions: Who? What? Where? When? Why? How? Journalists often use this technique.

If I wrote bullet points, it might look like this:

WHO:

- 3 little pigs
- big bad wolf

WHAT: houses

- straw – blew down
- sticks – blew down
- bricks – stayed

HOW: huff, puff, blow house down

WHY: moral of story: extra effort pays off, do it right the first time.

(Where and when is not so important in this particular story, as the events happened somewhere once upon a time).

Constructing the same information as a memory map might look like this:

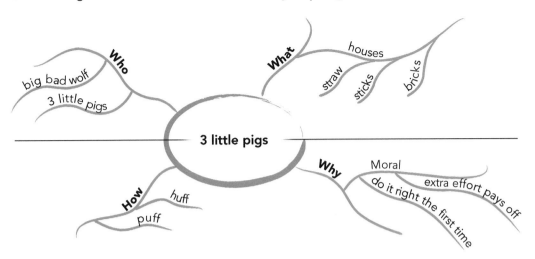

(Traditional notes vs. mapping)

Some people tell me at first glance: 'Memory maps are not for me. They look disorganised!' That might be true for them.

A memory map drawn by your own hand makes more sense, and gives better memory recall, than one drawn by someone else. To make a judgement about whether to use memory maps or not is best made after trialling a few, done freehand.

I've enjoyed using and gained value from them for all my learning and thinking and brainstorming and goal-setting for many years. I urge you to give them a try before dismissing them.

Ways to make a memory map more memorable

1. **Keywords** are quick, cultivate active listening and act as a memory trigger. Limit your notes to keywords or short phrases, as our brain finds it easier to remember key ideas rather than full sentences.

2. Use **colour** to enhance memory by association.

3. As well as starting in the centre then adding branches and keywords, **print** the words on each branch rather than use handwriting.

   Printing has more clarity on the page than handwriting, which means your brain is more likely to take a mental photograph of your memory map.

   When you try to recall, you may find you spontaneously picture in your mind a mental image of your memory map, so that when recalling you read your mental image.

   So printing the words makes your memory map more 'visual'.

What makes memory maps?

4. Create **headings** with impact by using two-dimensional lettering or putting boxes or shapes around the words.

5. **Icons** next to keywords are easy, fun and memorable, for example:
   - light bulb to indicate a good idea
   - key shape to indicate a key idea
   - book to reference one to read, and so on.

6. Leave lots of **white space** between branches. Don't try to cram too much information on one page.

7. You might prefer to use unlined paper.

8. The **landscape orientation** opens up the page. (We discussed this in Chapter 2.)

9. And remember to make it **fun!**

Here is an advanced version of the 8-step wheel incorporating memory mapping for notes.

Brainpower Smart Study 8-step method

1 – **Preview** for the big picture

2 – **Memory map outline** using key headings

3 – **Read** for understanding

4 – **Reread** a little faster

5 – **Postview**

6 – **Start memory map** – first from memory

7 – **Add memory map** – open-book, use another colour

Take ten

8 – **Retell**

Advanced version

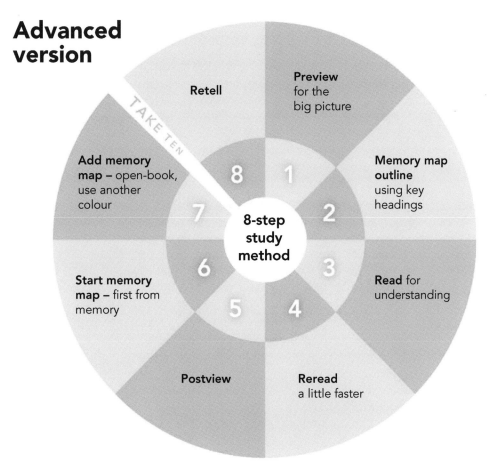

CHAPTER 14

USING THE TESTING EFFECT IN A DISCUSSION GROUP

Plan time with fellow students to collaborate and self-test using various tactics.

STUDENTS WHO WORK IN STUDY discussion groups learn better than students who work on their own.

How much better? Some research suggests it might be as much as 50% better.[1]

What would that mean in exam results? It might translate as an 87% mark instead of 75%.

Study groups are best kept fairly small, perhaps no more than 5 to 7 members. It's also a good idea to have a rotating leader. Many students already use live chat.

Here are a couple of ideas of ways to study in your group.

Review quiz

This is a fun activity you can use in a discussion group of three or more students meeting face to face.

1. Decide ahead of time the topic for discussion. Everyone arrives having read and studied the section. Alternatively, you can allocate time at the start for study.

2. Allow 5 minutes for each person to devise 5 or 6 or more quiz questions about the topic. The point is not to ask the most obscure question to which no one knows the answer, but the most relevant question, about something everyone needs to know.

3. Similar to quiz shows you may have seen on TV, each member of the group can bring a bell, buzzer, party blowout or other noise maker which they sound if they think they know the answer to a question asked. Alternatively, making a vocal sound is fine. The first person to sound their buzzer wins the right to answer the question. If they get it wrong, remaining members of the group may buzz in again for another chance to answer the question.

4. Take it in turns to ask your question to the group (whether or not you know the answer).

5. It doesn't matter whether you keep score. That's up to you.

This fun activity is usually accompanied by laughter.

Jigsaw method[2]

Divide the material to be remembered into parts like a jigsaw puzzle and allow a specific amount of time for each individual to learn their unique section, using the 8-steps. (You can either allow time at the start of the meeting or instruct everyone to study beforehand.)

Each member then teaches their part to the rest of the group, allowing for discussion and questions, until everyone has learned it all.

Tip: This makes a great 48-hour or 7-day review method.

►CHAPTER 15
NOW TEACH SOMEONE

NOW THAT YOU'VE READ THIS BOOK, go back and reread each chapter, do each of the eight steps referring to the 8-step wheel, then find a friend to tell them about the 8-step study method.

You learn best by teaching it. Take a look at the Learning Pyramid[1], below.

Learning Pyramid

The Learning Pyramid diagram below shows the deepest learning comes from using new information immediately **by teaching someone else.**

One reason I became a skilled speed reader was that soon after I attended the course I was invited to train to become an instructor. Teaching it encouraged me to not only keep using the skill but to master it.

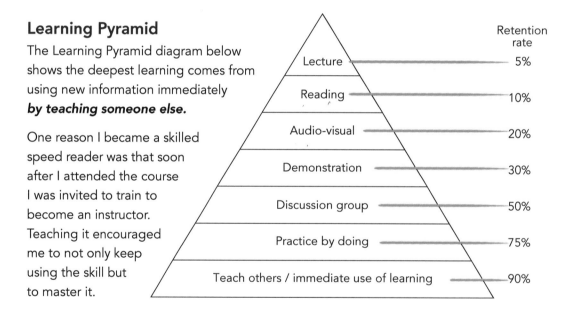

	Retention rate
Lecture	5%
Reading	10%
Audio-visual	20%
Demonstration	30%
Discussion group	50%
Practice by doing	75%
Teach others / immediate use of learning	90%

Chapter Summary

Now teach someone

1. Reread this book and teach each chapter to at least two fellow students.
2. Use the 8-step method when studying.
3. Form a discussion group for collaborative learning. Encourage every member of that discussion group to use the 8-step study method. Bring your notes or memory maps to your meetings.
4. Record and compare your exam results before and after using the 8-step method.

CHAPTER 16

SELF-TALK

How you talk to yourself can help you stay calm and confident.

BEING FOCUSED WHEN STUDYING FOR exams is important. And a big part of being focused is staying relaxed and confident.

What thoughts go through your mind during study or leading up to the exam? What do you tell your friends?

Negative self-talk includes statements such as:

- 'I'm going to fail.'
- 'Studying is hard.'
- 'I hate studying.'
- 'I'm not smart enough.'

You can choose your attitude. And your attitude springs from your self-talk. Whenever you catch yourself thinking negatively, simply replace that thought with a positive one. Tell yourself instead:

- 'I can do this.'
- 'I'm going to pass easily.'
- 'I now enjoy studying.'

On the day of the exam, just before entering the room, don't stand with anyone caught up in pre-exam panic, furiously skimming their notes or referring to textbooks. It just stresses you out.

Keep yourself in an emotionally neutral state of feeling calm and confident.

During the exam, if you can't recall an item, instead of thinking, 'I have forgotten it', tell yourself, 'It will come to me later'. A part of your brain can keep searching for an answer even while you are focused on answering the next question. This is an important reason why the first ten minutes or so of an exam is often spent reading and thinking about the whole paper before putting pen to paper.

An athlete surrenders to the discipline of daily training because they hold their end goals in sight. Consider yourself a mental athlete in daily training for your upcoming event, the test or exam. Hold your end goals in your mind – not only great test results but also the doors that open as a result.

►CHAPTER 17
LEARNING A SCRIPT USING SELF-TESTING

Try this method for memorising a drama script.

I RECENTLY COACHED A STUDENT WHO had to memorise and be ready to deliver to her class a one-page monologue from a play. Here's how we approached that task.

I asked her to identify the one memorable keyword in each sentence, and write each one down, vertically, as in a list.

For example, if memorising the first six lines from Puck's monologue at the end of Shakespeare's Midsummer Night's Dream[1]:

> PUCK
>   If we shadows have offended,
>   Think but this, and all is mended,
>   That you have but slumb'red here
>   While these visions did appear.
>   And this weak and idle theme,
>   No more yielding but a dream,

Rewrite the most memorable keyword in each line vertically in a list:

> shadows
> mended
> slumb'red
> visions
> theme
> yielding

Memorise these keywords to trigger the other words around them. If you can visualise what you are remembering, that's good.

Memorable keywords

Of course, you might prefer 'offended' rather than 'shadows' or 'dream' rather than 'yielding'. The word you choose should be the one that triggers **your** memory of the line, so there's no right or wrong word. You want the most meaningful and memorable word for you.

Then, learn the text using a similar method to the classic memory game where each person adds a new item to the list to be remembered:

I went to the shop and bought an apple.

I went to the shop and bought an apple and some bread.

I went to the shop and bought an apple, bread and a carrot.

I went to the shop and bought an apple, bread, a carrot and some donuts.

I went to the shop and bought an apple, bread, a carrot, donuts and some eggs.

And so on.

Add on as you go

1. Learn line 1 until you can retrieve it effortlessly from memory, using the keyword to trigger your memory of the rest of the line.

2. Learn line 2 until you can retrieve it effortlessly from memory, using the keyword to trigger your memory of the rest of the line.

3. Test you can retrieve lines 1 and 2 together effortlessly from memory. (If you can visualise what you are remembering, that's good.)

4. Learn line 3 until you can retrieve it effortlessly from memory.

5. Test you can retrieve lines 1, 2 and 3 together effortlessly from memory.

6. Learn line 4 until you can retrieve it effortlessly from memory.

7. Test you can retrieve lines 1–4 together effortlessly from memory.

8. Learn line 5 until you can retrieve it effortlessly from memory.

9. Test you can retrieve lines 1–5 together effortlessly from memory.

10. Learn line 6 until you can retrieve it effortlessly from memory.

11. Test you can retrieve lines 1–6 together effortlessly from memory.

Reward yourself

12. Now reward yourself with a short break of ten minutes – take ten.

Self-test

13. Test you can retrieve lines 1 to 6 effortlessly from memory. If not, go back to step 1 and relearn until you can.

14. Repeat the first 13 steps to memorise the next 6 lines of Puck's monologue.

> Gentles, do not **reprehend**.
> if you **pardon,** we will mend.
> And, as I am an **honest** Puck,
> If we have unearned **luck**
> Now to 'scape the **serpent's** tongue,
> We will make **amends** ere long;

I've made bold what I consider to be the memorable keywords to write vertically in a list and to memorise. Remember, you might select different keywords. The choice is yours. It's what you find meaningful and memorable.

15. Test you can remember both chunks together, first 6 lines and second 6 lines. If not, go back and relearn until you can.

Continue to learn the rest of the script using this method, learning in chunks followed by short breaks.

Glossary

active reading – marking the text with a pencil, pen or highlight pen as you read to identify important points

context – words surrounding an idea giving it meaning

critical thinking – ability to interact with the material, to make connections, to see relationships between ideas

exponential – growing increasingly larger at an increasingly faster rate

fixation – the number of words you see at one time as you read. For the average reader, that's one or two words at a time

gist – the main or essential part of the matter; a general idea of what it's all about

hindsight – to understand the significance of an event after it has happened

Macroreading® - scanning text with a relaxed eye focus at a rate around twice as fast as a comfortable reading rate, to gain an overview

memory map – a diagramming technique for notes using branches, keywords and colour, radiating from a central idea

mono-tasking – focusing on one task at a time

multi-tasking – doing more than one task at the same time

sub-vocalisation – mentally hearing the sound of the words as you read

References

The quotes, anecdotes and ideas described in this book were accumulated from a variety of sources over a number of years. While we've made every attempt to fully attribute the origin of each of these items, the author may have been unable to list some sources in the detail preferred.

INTRODUCTION

1. Baddeley, Alan D, *The Psychology of Memory*, p. 288. Harper & Row, London, 1985.
2. Glover, John A., 'The Testing Phenomenon. Not gone but nearly forgotten', in *Journal of Educational Psychology*, vol. 81, pp. 392-99. September 1989.

   Cranney, Jacquelyn, Ahn, Mihyun, McKinnon, Rachel, Morris, Sue, Watts, Kaaren. 'The testing effect, collaborative learning, and retrieval-induced facilitation in a classroom setting.' *European Journal of Cognitive Psychology*, 21, 919-940. September 2009.
3. Johnson, Cheryl I, and Mayer, Richard E, 'A testing effect with multimedia learning' in *Journal of Educational Psychology*, vol 101(3), pp. 621–29. August 2009.
4. Robinson, Francis Pleasant, *Effective Study* (4th edn), Harper & Row, 1970, first published 1946.

GETTING STARTED

1. Gould, J.D., Alfaro L, Barnes, V., Finn, R., Grischkowsky, N and Minuto, A, 'Reading is slower from CRT displays than from paper: attempts to isolate a single-variable explanation', *Human Factors*, *29(3)*, pp. 269-99. June 1987.
2. Gerald M. Edelman, MD, PhD, President of The Neurosciences Institute, San Diego, USA. www.nsi. edu. Winner of the 1972 Nobel Prize for Physiology or Medicine. Radio Interview, ABC Radio National, 'All in the mind' program, 'Consciousness, creativity and neural Darwinism', 2 February, 2011. www.abc.net.au/rn

CHAPTER 1: BIG PICTURE

1. Macroreading® is a registered trademark of Brainpower Training Pty Ltd, www.brainpowertraining.com.au.

CHAPTER 2: RECALL OUTLINE

1. Miller, George A, 'The Magical Number Seven, Plus or Minus Two: Some Limits on Our Capacity for Processing Information' in *Psychological Review*, vol. 63, pp. 81–97. 1956.

CHAPTER 3: ABSORB

1. Bretzing, Burke H, and Kulhary, Raymond W, 'Notetaking and depth of processing' in *Contemporary Educational Psychology*, 4 (2), pp. 145–53. April 1979.
2. For a good discussion on how to mark a book while reading, read this classic: Mortimer, Adler J, and Van Doven, Charles. *How to Read a Book: The Classic Guide to Intelligent Reading*, Touchstone Books, pp. 48–50. 1972.

CHAPTER 6: IMMEDIATE RECALL

1. Anatole France (1844-1924) was a French novelist who won the Nobel Prize for literature in 1921.
2. Baddeley, Alan D, *The Psychology of Memory*, p. 288. Harper & Row, London, 1985.
3. Johnson, Cheryl I and Mayer, Richard E, 'A testing effect with multimedia learning' in *Journal of Educational Psychology*, vol 101(3), pp. 621–29. August 2009.

CHAPTER 8: TAKE TEN

1. Newman, Aubrey S, *Follow Me 1: Human Element in Leadership*. Presidio Press. 1996.
2. Fields, R Douglas, 'Making Memories Stick' in *Scientific American* 292(2), pp. 74-81. February 2005.

CHAPTER 9: CONVERSATION

1. Baddeley, Alan D, *The Psychology of Memory*, p. 288. Harper & Row, London, 1985.
2. Gambrell, Linda B, Pfeiffer, Warren R and Wilson, Robert M, 'The effect of retelling upon comprehension and recall of text information' in *Journal of Educational Research* 78(4), pp. 216–20. 1985.

   Rose, MC, Cundick, BP and Higbee, KL, 'Verbal Rehearsal and Visual Imagery: Mnemonic Aids For Learning-Disabled Children' in *Journal of Learning Disabilities*, vol. 16, pp. 352-54. 1983.

   Gambrell, Linda B, Koskinen, Patricia S, and Kapinus, Barbara A, 'Retelling and the Reading Comprehension of Proficient and Less-Proficient Readers' in *Journal of Educational Research* 84(6), pp. 356-63. 1991.

   Morrow, LM, Gambrell, Linda B, Koskinen, Patricia S, Kapinus, Barbara A, Marshall, N and Mitchell, JN, 'Retelling: A strategy for reading instruction and assessment', in Dr. Jerry Niles and Dr. Rosary Lalik, (eds.), 'Solving problems in literacy: Learners, teachers and researchers', pp 73-80. New York: National Reading Conference. 1986.

CHAPTER 10: REGULAR REVIEW

1. Ebbinghaus, H, *'Über das Gedächtnis'* (translated as 'Memory. A Contribution to Experimental Psychology'). 1885. Self-conducted experiments describing the processes of learning and forgetting.

2. Fields, R Douglas, 'Making Memories Stick' in *Scientific American* 292(2), pp. 74-81. February 2005.

CHAPTER 12: MNEMONICS

1. Pluto is no longer regarded as a planet. At a meeting of the International Astronomical Union (IAU) in 2006 in Prague in the Czech Republic it was voted to consider Pluto not a true planet but a dwarf planet. This decision by the IAU has created some controversy.

CHAPTER 13: MEMORY MAPPING FOR NOTES

1. Mind Map® and Mind Maps® are registered trademarks of The Buzan Organisation and ThinkBuzan. www.thinkbuzan.com

2. Ishikawa, K. *'What is Total Quality Control? The Japanese Way'*, Transl. by J. Lu, 1985, Prentice-Hall.

3. 'Three Little Pigs and the Big Bad Wolf' was first published about 1843 in *Nursery Rhymes and Nursery Tales* by James Orchard Halliwell-Phillipps.

CHAPTER 14: USING THE TESTING EFFECT IN A DISCUSSION GROUP

1. Sampson, Victor and Clark, Douglas, 'The Impact of Collaboration on the Outcomes of Scientific Augmentation' in *Science Education* 93(3), pp. 448–84. May 2009.

2. The jigsaw classroom was first used in 1971 in Austin, Texas by Professor Elliot Aronson, Professor Emeritus, University of California, Santa Cruz. www.jigsaw.org

CHAPTER 15: NOW TEACH SOMEONE

1. The Learning Pyramid was developed in the 1960s by the National Training Laboratories (NTL), Institute for Behavioral Science, Bethel, Maine campus, and now NTL Institute for Applied Behavioral Science, Arlington, VA, USA. www.ntl.org

CHAPTER 17: LEARNING A SCRIPT USING SELF-TESTING

1. William Shakespeare (1564-1616), 'A Midsummer Night's Dream', Act V, Scene II.

    You can read 'A Midsummer Night's Dream' and the Complete Works of William Shakespeare at: Project Gutenberg, www.gutenberg.org

Acknowledgements

Thanks and appreciation to everyone who contributed their talents to this project in one way or another.

Joy Lankshear, Helena Bond, Paul Hassing, Russell, Ann and James Perks, Tony Ryan, Sarah Harris, Jo Daines, Stephanie Daines, Bobby Fleck, Andrea Bedelis, Shaun Lee, Melanie Mclean, Alex Mclean, Tom Loomes, Logesh Palanikumar, Danny Kenny, Charles Province from The Patton Society, Montana Hein.

SHARE IT WITH OTHERS

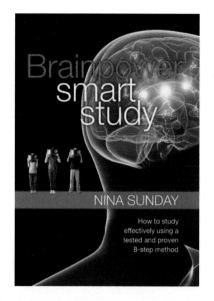

EVERY
STUDENT
NEEDS
TO READ
THIS BOOK

You may order more print copies of this book at discount.
Contact HowToStudyMethod.com for current price.

Single Copy: $_____ per copy + $_____ postage and handling _____

10+ Copies: $_____ per copy + $_____ postage and handling _____

25+ Copies: $_____ per copy + $_____ postage and handling _____

100+ Copies: $_____ per copy+ $_____ postage and handling _____

Special price quotes available for orders of 500 or more.

To instantly download the .pdf version visit:
www.HowToStudyMethod.com

Card type: ☐ Visa ☐ MasterCard

Card number: ☐☐☐☐ ☐☐☐☐ ☐☐☐☐ ☐☐☐☐ Expiry date: ☐☐ / ☐☐

Name on card_____ Signature_____

Name_____

E-mail_____

Address_____

_____ State_____ Zip/postcode_____

Tel_____ Fax_____

Brainpower Training Pty Ltd | ABN 63 064 883 932
HowToStudyMethod.com

CPSIA information can be obtained
at www.ICGtesting.com
Printed in the USA
LVIC01n1725190214
374384LV00018B/107